THE HISTORY OF THE CAROLINA PANTHERS

THE HISTORY OF THE

CAROLINA

Published by Creative Education

123 South Broad Street

Mankato, Minnesota 56001

Creative Education is an imprint of The Creative Company.

DESIGN AND PRODUCTION BY **EVANSDAY DESIGN**

LIBRARY OF CONGRESS CATALOGING-IN-PUBLICATION DATA

Goodman, Michael E.

The history of the Carolina Panthers / by Michael E. Goodman.

p. cm. — (NFL today)

Summary: Traces the history of the team from its beginnings through 2003.

ISBN 1-58341-290-5

1. Carolina Panthers (Football team)—History—Juvenile literature. [1. Carolina

Panthers (Football team)—History. 2. Football—History.] I. Title. II. Series.

GV956.C27G67 2004

796.332'64'09756—dc22   2003065100

First edition

9 8 7 6 5 4 3 2 1

COVER PHOTO: defensive end Julius Peppers

PANTHERS

Michael E. Goodman

NORTH CAROLINA AND SOUTH CAROLINA TODAY OCCUPY AN AREA THAT WAS ONCE PART OF A SINGLE COLONY SETTLED BY ENGLISH PLANTATION OWNERS IN THE 1660S. THE OWNERS NAMED THE COLONY CAROLINA, A LATIN VERSION OF THE NAME OF THE ENGLISH RULER, KING CHARLES II. IN 1729, THE COLONY WAS DIVIDED INTO TWO SECTIONS THAT LATER BECAME TWO STATES. WHILE EACH STATE TODAY HAS ITS OWN IDENTITY, THE TWO HAVE MAINTAINED CLOSE CONNECTIONS OVER THE YEARS. A NEW CONNECTION WAS ESTABLISHED IN 1993, WHEN THE NATIONAL FOOTBALL LEAGUE (NFL) AWARDED AN EXPANSION FRANCHISE TO THE REGION. TEAM OWNER JERRY RICHARDSON, A FORMER NFL PLAYER WHO WAS RAISED IN NORTH CAROLINA AND WENT TO COLLEGE IN SOUTH CAROLINA, WANTED THE TEAM TO REPRESENT BOTH STATES. HOPING THE TEAM WOULD HAVE THE SPEED AND POWER OF A BIG CAT, RICHARDSON NAMED IT THE CAROLINA PANTHERS.

JERRY RICHARDSON BEGAN making plans for a professional football team in the Carolinas in 1987. That was when NFL owners announced a competition to determine which two regions would be awarded expansion franchises in the league. Richardson and his son Mark approached several business executives in Charlotte, North Carolina, and convinced them to be part of a funding plan for a regional Carolina team.

Richardson was well-known in the region as both an outstanding football player and a successful businessman. In the late 1950s, Richardson was a star wide receiver at tiny Wofford College in Spartanburg, South Carolina.

He was drafted by the world champion Baltimore Colts and surprised many experts by making the team and then outshining all Colts rookies in 1959. He even caught a touchdown pass in Baltimore's 31–16 victory over the New York Giants in the NFL title game that year. "That pass has become legendary—in the Richardson family," he noted with a smile.

Each Colts player received $3,500 as a winner's bonus, and Richardson decided to invest his money. He joined with a friend to buy the first Hardee's restaurant franchise, which opened in Spartanburg in October 1961. Richardson then retired from football to concentrate on what would become a very successful business career.

Pro football continued to occupy a prominent place in Richardson's heart, however, and he began thinking about owning a team that would represent both North and South Carolina. After six years of hard work behind the scenes, Richardson's dream came true. In October 1993, the NFL's expansion committee announced that the Carolina Panthers would become one of two new franchises to begin league play in 1995. The Jacksonville Jaguars were added a few months later.

HAVING SECURED A franchise, Richardson had less

than two years to assemble a team. He started by hiring

veteran football man Bill Polian as the club's first gen-

eral manager. Polian had previously helped transform

the Buffalo Bills from one of the worst teams in the

American Football Conference (AFC) to a four-time AFC

champion. But after the Bills lost their fourth consecu-

tive Super Bowl in 1993, Polian was fired. The Panthers

jumped at the chance to bring him on board.

Cornerback Rod Smith (number 35) provides veteran leadership during Karolina's opening season.

Known for his intelligence, linebacker Sam Mills anchored the defense in Carolina's first season.

Polian had two key jobs: to hire the team's first coach, and to put together the club's first roster by selecting players in the expansion and college drafts and signing up free agents. Polian decided that a young, inexperienced team would need a disciplined coach, and he made an offer to Pittsburgh Steelers defensive coordinator Dom Capers. What most impressed Polian about the 44-year-old Capers was his work ethic. No one put in more hours working on the field or studying game films than Capers. "Football is a way of life," Capers once said. "However long it takes to get the job done, we'll do it. The most important thing is for us to be as well-prepared on Sunday as we can be."

Together, Polian and Capers put the first Panthers team together. Choosing from a list of players made available from the other NFL teams in an expansion draft, Carolina selected such proven players as cornerbacks Rod Smith and Tim McKyer, receiver Mark Carrier, and defensive tackle Greg Kragen.

The Panthers' front office next looked to the 1995 NFL Draft for a young quarterback who would be the team's offensive leader of the future. Their choice was big (6-foot-5 and 240 pounds) and talented passer Kerry Collins, who had led Penn State University to an undefeated season in 1994. Collins had impressed talent scouts with his size, arm strength, leadership skills, and poise.

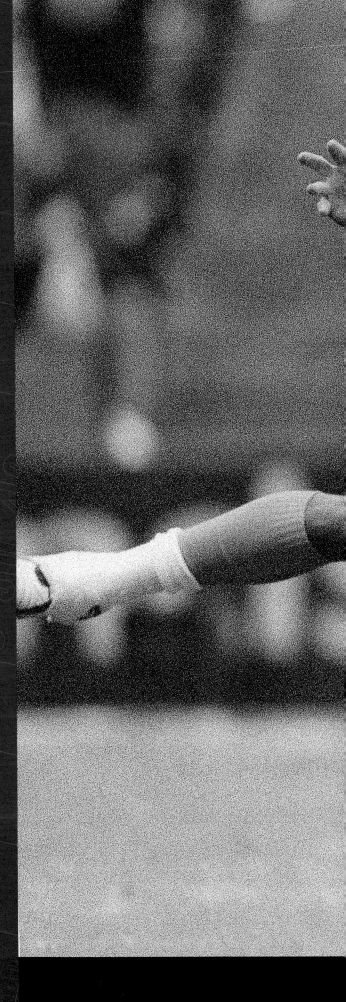

But Polian was concerned that Collins might not be ready to face NFL defenses right away. So he signed Frank Reich, the backup quarterback on all four Buffalo Bills Super Bowl teams, as a free agent. The plan was for Reich to be the starter until Collins was ready to step in. Other free-agent pickups included linebackers Lamar Lathon and Sam Mills, safety Brett Maxie, and placekicker John Kasay. These players made up a solid veteran core for the new team as it prepared to play its first NFL season.

NO ONE WAS SURPRISED when the Panthers got off to a 0–5 start in 1995. Fans and experts were amazed, however, when Carolina then won its next four games in a row. The most impressive win was a stunning 13–7 upset of the defending Super Bowl champion 49ers in San Francisco. By the season's end, the Panthers had set a record for first-year NFL teams with a 7–9 record.

During the Panthers' winning streak, Collins took over at quarterback and quickly proved he was no ordinary rookie, passing for more than 2,700 yards and 14 touchdowns. His favorite target that year was veteran receiver Mark Carrier, who snagged 66 passes for 1,002 yards. "Mark is an old pro, and when things would break down, I always knew where to find him," said Collins. "He was my security blanket out there."

Even as a rookie, Kerry Collins impressed teammates and fans with his accurate, high-velocity passes.

The club's defensive stars that first season were linebacker Sam Mills and safety Brett Maxie. Mills led the club in tackles and made several key interceptions, including one that sealed the Panthers' first victory, a 26–15 win over the New York Jets. Maxie led a ball-hawking secondary that often gave opposing receivers fits.

If the Panthers' first-season results were surprising, their second-year performance was astounding. The club opened the 1996 season in the brand-new, 73,000-seat Ericsson Stadium in Charlotte, North Carolina. The new stadium was a big improvement over the team's first-year home, the stadium on the campus of Clemson University in South Carolina. The entrances to the new field were guarded by six massive bronze panthers whose fierce expressions let visiting teams know they were in for a fight. "I love the big cats," said Carolina offensive tackle Blake Brockermeyer. "They make the place look mean."

Opponents soon learned just how mean the Panthers were in their new home. Carolina went undefeated in eight regular-season games at Ericsson Stadium on its way to a stunning 12–4 record. Playing in front of sellout crowds, the Panthers usually blew out opponents by double-digit margins. "From the time you walk into this place, you feel invincible," said Panthers linebacker Kevin Greene. "The fans won't let us lose."

The Panthers finished the 1996 season with seven straight wins and roared into the playoffs. They defeated the Dallas Cowboys before losing to the powerful Green Bay Packers in the National Football Conference (NFC) championship game. Carolina fans warmly greeted the team plane when it landed at the airport in Charlotte following the defeat. Addressing the crowd, Sam Mills echoed the fans' feelings when he said, "It hurts to lose, but I'm so proud of these guys."

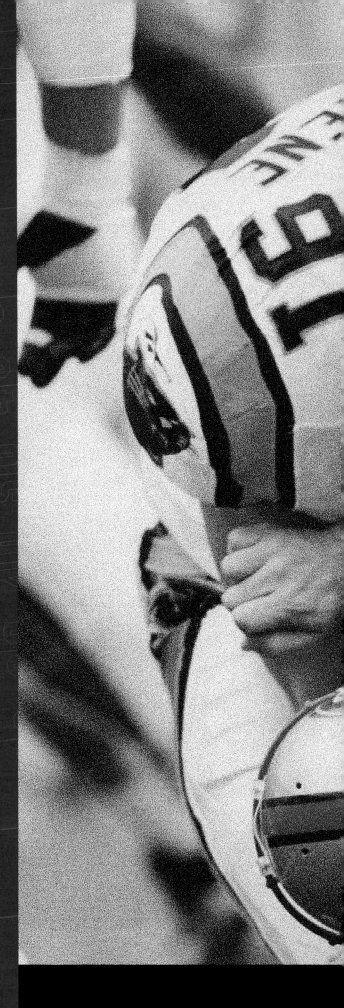

Green Bay's linebacker Kevin Greene chased down opposing quarterbacks for 14.5 sacks in 1996.

SEIFERT STOPS THE SLUMP>

AFTER THE PANTHERS' amazing start, Carolina fans were hoping for even greater achievements in Ericsson Stadium in the late 1990s. They were disappointed, however. Despite the solid play of Pro-Bowlers such as tight end Wesley Walls and kick returner Michael Bates, the club slid quickly down the NFC standings. The Panthers' record slipped to 7–9 in 1997 and then to 4–12 in 1998 when injuries and player disputes destroyed the team's winning chemistry.

Kerry Collins, who began to struggle with alcohol abuse problems, was released midway through the 1998 season and replaced at quarterback by veteran Steve Beuerlein. While Beuerlein made a strong showing, the Carolina defense had a terrible year. After the season, Dom Capers was fired as head coach and replaced by George Seifert,

Wesley Walls tied an NFL record for tight ends with 12 touchdown catches during the 1999 season.

Muhsin Muhammad was a big, physical wide receiver ^

Michael Barrow made a team-leading 111 tackles in 1999 ^

who had previously led the San Francisco 49ers to two Super Bowl wins. When the Panthers approached Seifert, who was then working as a broadcaster, about taking the coaching reins, he jumped at the chance. "I'm so excited to be coaching again," he told reporters. "This organization is committed to winning, and it's my job to make sure that happens."

Looking over his new team, Seifert was impressed with some of the offensive talent already in place. This included Beuerlein, Walls, running back Tim Biakabutuka, and wide receiver Muhsin Muhammad. Coach Seifert also saw the makings of a strong defense in such players as linebacker Michael Barrow, safety Mike Minter, and tackle Sean Gilbert.

After his new team got off to a 2–5 start in 1999, Seifert began making changes that turned the club around. The Panthers won six of their last nine games, just missing the playoffs. Beuerlein was the key to the dramatic turnaround. The veteran quarterback earned a trip to the Pro Bowl by throwing for 4,436 yards and 36 touchdowns. "It was a great run for us," said Beuerlein. "A lot of people wrote us off early in the year, but our guys kept scrapping."

UNFORTUNATELY, COACH SEIFERT was unable to achieve the same success in Carolina as he had in San Francisco. His Panthers played inconsistently in 2000, finishing 7–9. Then, in 2001, everything fell apart. The team underwent a shakeup before the season when Beuerlein left town as a free agent. Rookie quarterback Chris Weinke led Carolina to an opening week victory over the Minnesota Vikings, but that turned out to be the team's only win of the season. Over the next 15 weeks, the Panthers suffered late-game collapses, overtime losses, and occasional blow-outs. At the end of the 1–15 season, Seifert resigned.

Chris Warnke was a minor league baseball player before becoming an NFL rookie at the age of 27.

Down! Gray ⟨27⟩ Set! Hut!

John Fox quickly built the Panthers into a contender ^

Jake Delhomme led Carolina to its first Super Bowl ^

While the Panthers collapsed in 2001, the New York Giants were coming off a Super Bowl appearance, thanks in large part to the efforts of their defensive coordinator, John Fox. Before the 2002 season, the Panthers hired Fox to replace Seifert as head coach. Coming into his first Carolina training camp, Fox told his players that he expected them to do two things—work hard and have fun. He then repeated one of his favorite quotes: "This game is only fun when you win."

With an offense led by veteran quarterback Rodney Peete, and a defense anchored by 6-foot-6 and 280-pound rookie end Julius Peppers, the Panthers began having fun right from the start in 2002 and finished with a respectable 7–9 record. Fans were perhaps most excited watching Peppers's devastating pass rushes and hard tackles. "He's probably the most athletic guy I've played with since I've been in the league," said 10-year veteran defensive tackle Brentson Buckner.

With Peppers and fellow defensive end Mike Rucker on defense, Coach Fox improved the offense by signing running back Stephen Davis, wide receiver Ricky Proehl, and quarterback Jake Delhomme before the 2003 season. This collection of talent jelled much quicker than anyone expected. Thanks largely to a fierce defense and Davis's 1,444 rushing yards, the 2003 Panthers went 11–5. They then

Despite their tough Super Bowl loss, the Panthers have a bright future with such young stars as Mike Rucker.

shocked the sports world by toppling the Dallas Cowboys, St. Louis Rams, and Philadelphia Eagles in the playoffs to reach the Super Bowl.

The Panthers faced the New England Patriots in what turned out to be one of the most exciting Super Bowls in history. Delhomme did his best to lead the underdog Panthers to victory, throwing for 323 yards and three touchdowns and giving Carolina a 22–21 lead in the fourth quarter. Unfortunately, a Patriots field goal with four seconds left sent the Panthers to a heartbreaking 32–29 defeat. Still, Coach Fox could not have been prouder of his players and their extraordinary season. "It's been a great ride," he told reporters. "We just came up a little short. We have a lot to build on."

After a rollercoaster ride up and down the NFC standings in the late 1990s, the Carolina Panthers have again fought their way back to the top. The club that set league records as an expansion franchise not so long ago is today hoping to settle permanently among the NFL's elite teams. As the Panthers continue to fight for a world championship, fans in both North and South Carolina may soon have plenty to roar about.

INDEX >